LIBRARY of AMERICA

Ursula K. Le Guin's

Book of Cats

Published in the United States by Library of America,
14 East 60th Street, New York, NY 10022.
Visit our website at www.loa.org.

Back cover quote from Ursula K. Le Guin, "Dogs, Cats,
and Dancers: Thoughts About Beauty," in *The Wave in
The Mind: Talks and Essays on the Writer, the Reader, and the
Imagination* (2024).

Cover, cursive on title page and pages 23 and 96,
coloring and book design © Isabel Urbina Peña.

Distributed to the trade in the United States by
Penguin Random House Inc.
and in Canada by Penguin Random House Canada Ltd.

The authorized representative in the EU for
product safety and compliance is eucomply OÜ, Pärnu
mnt 139b-14, 11317 Tallinn, Estonia.
hello@eucompliancepartner.com

Library of Congress Control Number: 2025937865
ISBN 978–1–59853–829–8

Printed in the United States of America

1 3 5 7 9 10 8 6 4 2

CONTENTS

URSULA K. LE GUIN'S
BOOK *of* CATS

Ursula, c. 1933, with cats
at Napa Valley Ranch.

We human beings have made a world reduced to ourselves and our artifacts, but we weren't made for it and have to teach our children to live in it. Physically and mentally equipped to be at home in a richly various and unpredictable environment, competing and coexisting with creatures of all kinds, our children must learn poverty and exile, to live on concrete among endless human beings, seeing animals only as a bird high in the air, a beast on a leash or in a cage, a film image. But our innate, acute interest in animals as fellow beings, friend or enemy or food or playmate, can't be instantly eradicated; it resists deprivation. And imagination and literature are there to fill the void and reaffirm the greater community.

–*Cheek by Jowl,* Ursula K. Le Guin

THE ART OF

BUNDITSU

THE BUNDIT.

How to Arrange Your
Bonzo —

THE ART OF
BUNDITSU

A Form of Japanese
Tabbist Meditation

BY

Bunto Ursura

❧ Nekobooks ❧
1982

THE ART OF BUNDITSU

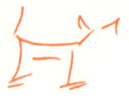

The Wild Bonzo comes in many
forms, all of which need
arranging.

A Suitable Vase,

with suggested
    Beginner's Arrangement.

THE ART OF BUNDITSU

三 八

An Advanced Arrangement.

. Subtlety is recommended in
the use of Whiskers.

THE ART OF BUNDITSU

Avoidance of Symmetry:

An Important

Principle.

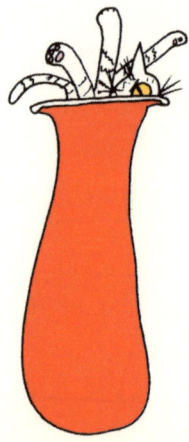

The Problem of the
Narrow Vase

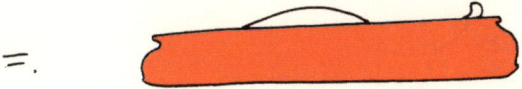

Two Solutions to the Low
Flat Pot Problem

Cold Weather Arrangement

(Without Vase)

On Mat

THE ART OF BUNDITSU

Hot Weather Arrangement:

Aesthetic Deployment
of Paws.

THE ART OF BUNDITSU

The Principle of
           Chastity.

The Principle of
Great Chastity

The Principle of
Perfect Chastity.

BLACK LEONARD IN NEGATIVE SPACE

All that surrounds the cat
is not the cat, is all
that is not the cat, is all,
is everything, except the animal.
It will rejoin without a seam
when he is dead. To know
that no-space is to know
what he does not, that time
is space for love and pain.
He does not need to know it.

FOR LEONARD, DARKO, AND BURTON
WATSON

A black and white cat
on May grass waves his tail, suns his belly
among wallflowers.
I am reading a Chinese poet
called The Old Man Who Does As He Pleases.
The cat is aware of the writing
of swallows
on the white sky.
We are both old and doing what pleases us
in the garden. Now I am writing
and the cat
is sleeping.
Whose poem is this?

TABBY LORENZO

The small cat smells of bitter rue
and autumn night. His ears are scarred.
His dark footpads are like hard flowers.
On my knee he rests entirely
trusting and entirely strange,
a messenger to all indoors
from the gardens of danger.

A CONVERSATION WITH A SILENCE

What kept you out so late my love?

I was running, I was running in the dark.

Dawn and raining when you came home.

The trees are clouds and roads to me.
I run the sweet dirt-darkness in the rain
and up where leafy chirping sleep-warmths
nestle their blood for me. I meet my enemies
below: the White One, the Singer.

What does your brother watch from the window?

Ghosts in the other garden.
I don't see ghosts. I go farther
along the cloud-roads
to kill where darkness branches in the rain.

DON DIEGO

Softly and furrily
proceeds he:
in catly fashion
he goes
where? who knows?
on pink cushion
and unhurriedly.

A LITTLE DEATH

His eyes did not see outward any more,
the gold gone dull behind the crystal spheres.
He lifted up his head and cried out twice,
loudly, to whom? and stretched himself, and died,
the small soul going forth with terrible grandeur.

Asked, "Hardy! what do cats say?" he'd reply,
obligingly, "Meow." That was his sop
to human vanity. The rest of pride
was his: his territory: sprayed, and held
by battle. He was white and orange, fat,
insolent and innocent and greedy,
a clumsy hunter and a potent sire.

He sent his life forth as the crippled tree
puts forth white flowers in April every year
upon the dying branch. He knew the way.

All cats are balloons.
All cats are Petunias.
All cats are mangold-wurzels.
All cats are Yin enough.
All cats guide me.

A U.K. Comic Book Regus. Pat. Off. ® 1994
SUPER MOUSE!
In the offices of the Daily Trashcan works a mild-mannered snaggletoothed young rat named Clark Clark
No one knows that Clark Clark needs only to put on his Magic Cloak to become
SUPERMOUSE!
Supermouse can see through cheese!
Cheese-Ray Vision
Supermouse laughs at Mousetraps!
HA! HA! HA!

☞ GREETINGS! ☜

NOTICE OF PERPETRATION.

This first issue of SUPERMOUSE
COMIX was drawn quite a
while ago by Ursula for Ted,
and then Jeff Levin got a
hold of it, so whose fault is
it, anyway?
Certainly not yours.

Balloon

and o

Postcards   by

cats

her fancies

Ursula

Ballooncats on a Windy Day

Ballooncats on a Quiet Day

Ballooncat Meeting

School of Balloonfish

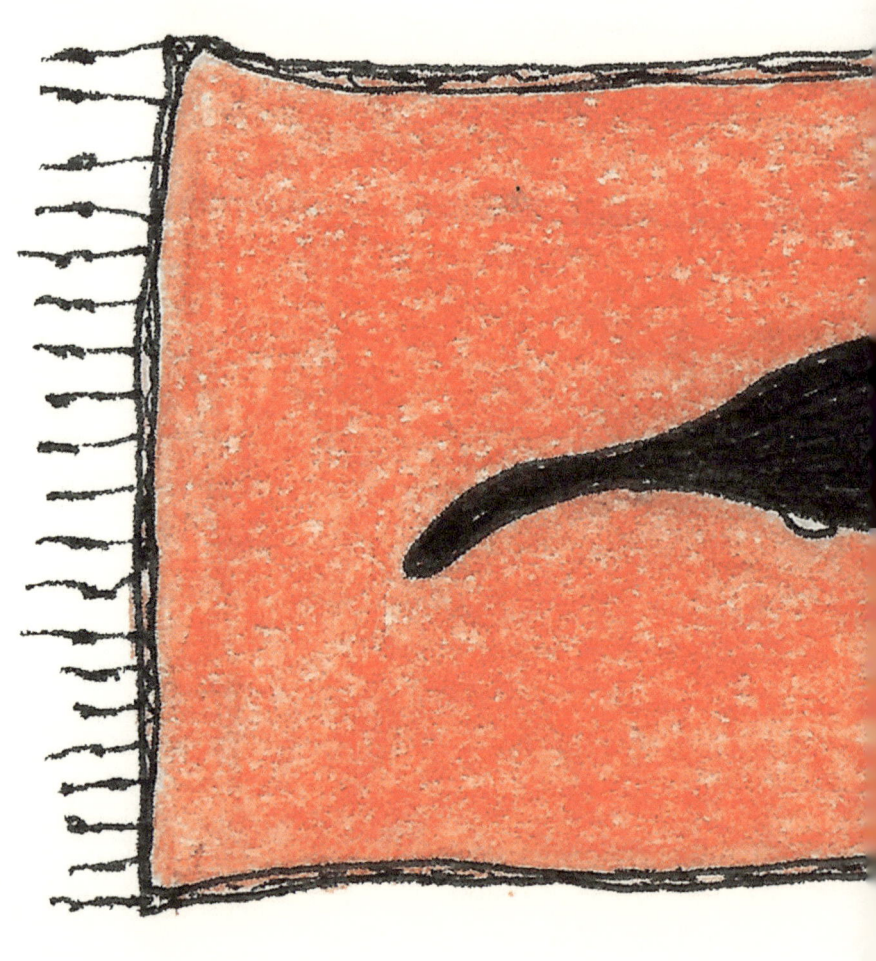

Black Cat with White Paws Proceeding

Cautiously Across Red Rug. Top View.

what did they do with

the other Cat ?

Cats in
Space

NEKO AT TWENTY

Old moth,
shadow,
sticks-in-silk,
wasted, swagbellied, hardscrabbler,
piss-in-the-corner, piss-and-tell,
loud yowler, greedy,
opaque and luminous gaze
fixed on longer than a cat can live
and keeping the secret:
no verb for you
but be,
be old,
old furbones,
moth,
shadow.

Neko
eating from Len's bowl

TO NEKO: TWO OLD LADIES
ON THE SAME BED

Move your big butt over.
    Cacackle mrrrm.
Oh come on, move over,
silly old piss-in-the-kitchen.
    Awww oww.
All right then take the whole bed.
See if I care.
    Prrrrnprrrnprrrnprrrrrnnprrrrrnnprrrrr

Nero
eating from Neko's bowe

SLEEPING WITH CATS

In smoothness of darkness are
warm lumps of silence.
There are no species.
Purring recurs.

x

45

CAT PHILIP

Philip looks like
my father. I think
I'm not supposed to notice.
It's in the jawline, yawning,
and the short neat beard.
    In old Neko arthritically
clumping downstairs,
yawping for dinner,
gazing into what world, I see
myself, but mere senility,
not family likeness.
    It seems I see my father oftener
these days so many years
farther from his death and nearer mine.
Philip was born
there, in that place.
All kinds of trading could go on
there
under the trees my father planted.

I wonder what I am supposed to notice.

FROM LORENZO

I feel that barred and mottled tabby
coat of fur fits me,
it's my claws fixed in that crabapple tree
and my gasoline green glare
on the bird above me.
My wings bear me from the bough
so lightly, and I feel
the bark and tender cambium
under it and my leaves playing
with the wind. I climb myself
and fly away.

LORENZO/ORION

My friend grows old. The fireside
draws him from the hunt,
the airy ways he used to run,
the wet, sweet coverts of the field mice.
His eyes, though golden,
are not what they were.
Seldom now the small, stiff gift
of vole or velvet mole, the pledge
of blood's realm mind bars me from,
where he reigns: innocent,
mortal, the only hunter in my heart.

LORENZO

A proud and purring silkiness.
Sixteen years veil
the fierce gold glare.
Neat thorny feet that catch
my heart.   This other mind
that gives me comfort,
teaches me peril.
He was born wild.
He has been
my silk, my gold, my wilderness.

ENTANGLEMENTS

MARCH 28
Black cat, amiable visitor,
let's give each other
all the pleasure we can, quick,
yes, sitting on each other
in the sunlight and stroking
each other with our hands and faces,
being warm and tender and enjoyable,
yes, we should enjoy each other
while we are in the sun together
because all my black cats here
die and my friend here
dies by his own hand that lifts
and lifts the glass and the sunlight
doesn't last long here
with the land-wind blowing
and blowing tender and relentless
to the salt abyss, no place
for a cat or a friendship.

NIGHT OF MARCH 28–29
Black cat don't twist my heart
around your crying
crouched at my door
with a dusty forehead, all night
crying and waiting for a person
who's no good to you.
Is a caress a promise?

Black cat I should be the one
making plans and you living wholly.
But you are making plans
without a future and my now
is twisted into your crying.

Yes sure I should have been able
to help somehow, I should be able
to help now somehow, something
more use than a pat on the shoulder
and Hi how's it going.

Is everything a promise?
Are all of them broken?

March 29
Black cat you are a fraud.
Your lady lives around the corner
and keeps her promises
or you wouldn't be the meaty
cat the hefty cat the bully cat
you are. A neighbor told me.
I should have listened to the crows
shouting Fraud! Fraud!
down from the phonepoles at you.
Pots calling the kettle.
You beat up his calico,
the neighbor said. Black hearted.
Bloody minded. A lesson to me.

Is everything a lesson?

Black is the lesson
I am learning from my friend.
How life gets twisted
until there's no way ever to untie it
because the future has become
the past and there is no now
no way. No way at all.

MARCH 30
No way to love usefully.

MARCH 31
Black cat you are a monster
wailing round the walls
and on the roof all night
crying and yowling let me in let me in
pet me pet me at three in the morning.
Caterwauling our modest affection
into a false inflated passion
a nonexistent drama of desertion
a little black misery. Oh why?
Why make us both miserable?
Why punish us? What for?
For sitting together in the sunlight?
What did we do wrong?

APRIL 4
Little demon of innocence,
the sun's shining, let's caress
again and sit on each other, yes,
let's hurry, yes, to offer
everything and count on nothing,
make and break no promises
and let no guilt
and no experience
come between the stroker and the stroked,
the offer and the offering.
Outside trust, what air
is there to breathe?

Cat T'ai chi

Quadruple Whip
("Reaching the Inaccessible")

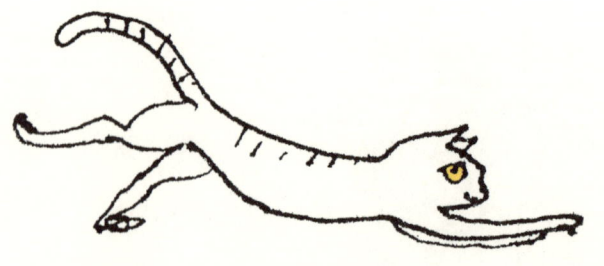

Extend One Paw to Rear
+ Stretch

Wash Eyebrows
Cutely

Squat Broadly
and Stare

Carry Kitten
to Mountain

Ursula with Lorenzo in 1996.

THE CAT LETTERS

(obediently transcribed by Elisabeth and Ursula Le Guin)

Although incomplete, these letters are of great interest in revealing much concerning the Five Deliberations.

Though practiced openly and constantly by most cats, the actual nature of the Deliberations has remained obscure to most humans. Frederika's revelation of them by name and her description of the practice to her correspondent Zorro is an epoch in our understanding of feline thought, and should clarify many mysteries of feline behavior.

At the time these letters were written, Zorro was about twelve, and had been in control of two humans in Portland, Oregon, for many years. Orphaned and abandoned as a kitten, he had had little or no teaching from elders of his kind, and had worked out a code of behavior of his own which was not always entirely satisfactory to himself or others. His epistolary friendship with Frederika was a great boon to him.

The growing bond between him and Opal was less intellectual, but of considerable interest also, particularly as regards their discussions of humping and biting.

Frederika, in middle age, was in full control of a single human, in West Hollywood, California. A somewhat troubling element had recently been introduced into her life in the person of Opal, a completely uneducated young cat, whose presence certainly caused Frederika to call upon the spirit and practice of the Deliberations more actively than ever. But it is clear that Frederika was an adept, a true sage, ready to teach any who called upon her for teaching—as Zorro did, though Opal unfortunately did not.

There are no pictures currently available of the three correspondents. Zorro always wore tuxedo. Frederika still dresses in subtle and becoming grey; Opal favors a mixture of rather gaudy colors including orange, white, and black.

The opening letters of the correspondence have been lost. It ended, sadly, with Zorro's death in 2011, only a few weeks after his last letter to Opal.

FIRST SERIES—DECEMBER 2010
Zorro to Opal and Frederika

Dear Opal and Frederika,
I wanted to tell you about the mouse I caught. I have let my humans catch the other mice, under the sink in the kitchen, because the mice have an escape hole there, but the humans have this box trap, and all I have to do is stand at the cabinet door and lash my tail and make my eyes into searchlights until they realise that there is a mouse in there and set the trap for it.

The mouse in the attic study was however more accessible to me and after long strategic planning I caught it by knocking over a wastebasket and a few other things in a prolonged, noise-producing, highly satisfying Chase Scene. I then brought it down to the front bedroom, where, naturally, I released it so it could play with me educationally. It played with me a little bit but then cheated and got down into the furnace grate and disappeared, which is unfair. They watched with great interest, I will say that for them, but I doubt they learned much. How can I teach them how to catch mice without traps if the mouse does not cooperate?

I ate the first mouse I ever caught and part of the second one but then decided that they are far more interesting and valuable educationally.

Wishing you asparagus, calf's liver, and sufficient ham,
Your Friend at a Distance,
Z

Frederika to Zorro

Dear Zorro,
Here in our big pink building we do not have mice. I have searched quite extensively. This is unfortunate, and I suspect foul play on the part of the humans. Opal clearly does not know what a mouse is; she is very young and ignorant; how is she to learn the basics???

There have, however, been birds on occasion. I remember with fondness the last, a young crow that I dismembered at leisure in the living room. The human living with me at that time was thoughtful enough to let me take all afternoon at it.* It is a pity Opal was not there at that time, it would have been a fine anatomy lesson.

However, there have not been birds of late and so I have entered upon the practice of the Five Deliberations.

---

* (Note from Human: This was my last tenant but one, Marianna, who wrote me about it while I was in Spain. She is an ardent vegan. She left the scene in dismay, and made her boyfriend clean it up.)

I was in the preliminary phases when Opal arrived, apparently to stay. This was fortuitous, since her youthful abysmal ignorance and silliness have provided me with much opportunity to intensify my practice of the Second Deliberation.**

I have few complaints. For some reason Opal's food tastes consistently better than my own, but this situation is easily remedied. Less easy to remedy is the Usual Human's consistent unwillingness to arise for the 4 AM Snack required by all true Practicants; but I have found a particular spot to scratch on the headboard of the bed which usually effects a response.

When this is inefficacious, I have been known to lick the tip of her nose. There is, of course, no personal affection implied, consistent with the Foundational Deliberation.***

On this windy night I send you all due Crunchy Treats, and a dollop of half-and-half,

Frederika

Opal to Zorro

Grrrrrr, grrrrrr
— Opal

** Ignoring.

*** Reserve.

Zorro to Frederika

Dear Frederika,

I am deep in admiration concerning the crow. I had
quite given up on birds since they have these stupid
front leg sort of things (even worse than the humans'
"arms") which they use to go up off into the air with. It is
abnormal and unjust.

My mouse used the Furnace Vent Routes and is now on
the ground floor, behind the stove. I spent most of the day
crouching and lashing my tail at his exit route. I am glad
that the humans have set their little trap there so that I can
go up to the blue chair and go to sleep, I have certainly
earned it.

I should like to know more of the Deliberations.

I have certain Practices. One of them I think resembles
your Headboard Scratching, but it is a little more direct;
it consists of Head Scratching. When the Female Human
is facing the wrong way in bed (lying on her left side) she
needs to be rearranged, so I come and scratch the top of
her head (quite gently, barely any claw extrusion at all)
until she turns over and faces the correct direction (lying
on her right side) so that I can lie down beside her pillow
with my butt in her face and go to sleep.

Head Scratching is quite effective. Has never failed yet.
You might try it.

Z.

Zorro to Opal

Dear Opal,
Hssssssssssssssss hsss.
Your Distant Friend,
Zorro

Frederika to Zorro

Dear Zorro,
Herewith the Five as I have been taught them. I hope that you find them useful.

1. Reserve (the Foundational Deliberation). A host of divergent translations reflect regional and philosophical variations: The Cat that Walks by Himself (Great Britain and former colonies); Self-Sufficiency (North America); Cat Tvam Asi (East Asia); and (among Japanese temple cats) Mu.

2. Ignoring.

3. The Warmth Asana (sometimes expressed as an equation, $x = 1/b2$, where x is the ambient temperature and b2 the amount of fur exposed to air). The physical calibrations required to maintain equilibrium can be enormously delicate in a mild climate such as that of my home.

4. Placement (Feng Shui). Finding the right place in which to practice, relative to current conditions (topography, temperature, astrological factors, misguided attempts at reading by humans).

5. Sameness. That things should be always the same goes without saying; maintaining Sameness in a world prone to

lamentable irregularities that are out of our control (I need only mention the terrible Cat Carrier) is said to be the highest discipline of them all. In a certain sense the first four Deliberations can be considered preliminary to the Fifth.

I wish a satisfying outcome to your labors with the mouse.
— Frederika

Opal to Zorro

I like playing with human underwear, do you?
— Opal

Zorro to Frederika

Dear Frederika,
I deeply admire your formulation of the Five Deliberations. It is clear that you have acquired true wisdom. As it is said, Adversity is the Mother of Felinity. I wish you, if Perfect Sameness is unattainable, at least a monotonous Regularity perturbed only by the slightest variations, such as the occasional crow.

The mouse has not evidenced itself recently, so I have retired to the attic furnace grate, which is covered by a carpet which spreads the heat out nicely, thus facilitating the Third Deliberation, and is also near the blue chair where the human sits making those misguided attempts to read from which, by judicious exercise of the Fourth Deliberation, I can often save him.

Your Friend, remotely,
Zorro

Zorro to Opal

Dear Opal:
No. I like humping fleece things while going oww,
wowww, do you?
Z.

Opal to Zorro

Dear Uncle Zorro,
Right now I am alone in my Private Place because I got
mad at Auntie Fredi and said bad things.

She made me mad because she wanted to go on the
human's lap but so did I. This was Not Fair. And then she
went up on a piece of furniture that was higher than
me and looked down on me all superior the way she does.
Her and her Deliberations, phhht. So I went in the middle
of the floor and looked away from everybody and made
my eyes all greeny and lashed my tail and said grrrr, grrrr,
ooowwwwooo.

And then when the human put me in the Private Place
I bit her. I am sorry for that part, but sometimes bites come
out and have to be bitten.

But now I am feeling better and softer and when the
human comes to the door she will bring me a treat
because she always does.

What is humping?
— Opal

Frederika to Zorro

I forgot to mention a refinement to the Fourth
Deliberation with which you are doubtless familiar; it
concerns computers and tails. With practice, and constant
delicate flicking adjustments, it is possible to cover a
surprising number of the keys that the human wants to
tap upon. This can often result in being invited, even
if somewhat ungently, onto the Lap. That is where I
currently reside.
— Fredi

P.S. Of course I do not look down on anyone even when
I am superior to them. I am Ignoring; but the ignorant do
not recognize this.

Zorro to Opal

Dear Young Opal,
You must not say phhht to your Aunt Fredi. Saying phhht
is excessively kittenish and you are not a kitten any more.
Consider, for example, that you have a Private Place, in
which you may withdraw, or be withdrawn, to practice
both the Foundational and the Great Fifth Deliberations at
leisure. Kittens have no Private Places except momentarily
inside cartons, drawers, cupboards, etc., and then another
kitten or two or six always crowds in, rendering Reserve
impossible and destroying all hope of Sameness. You are
a fortunate young Cat and should behave as such.

I entirely understand and approve of your philosophy of
bites. If I had not lost my lower fangs (when a foolish and

trusting youth, I was attacked by a viciously unstable small end-table), my own practice of the custom would be even more effective than it is. I favor the wrist, which bleeds most satisfactorily, do you?

As for humping, I feel perhaps you should consult your Aunt on this subject. It concerns gender, about which I find my ideas not as clear as I should like them to be. I know that gender is what divides us into Toms and Queens, but having begun life (I am quite certain) as a Tom kitten, I do not seem to be a Tom cat, yet am quite certain that I am not an old Queen. Perhaps fleece blankets and shirts do not have the peculiar fascination for you that they have for me, so I shall say no more about humping at this time.

I wish you excellent, crunchy, utterly undeserved treats.
Uncle Zorro

Zorro to Frederika

Dear Fredi,
Ah what poetry is in your saying: "I am Ignoring, but the ignorant do not recognise this." I deeply sympathise with your being required to live with a young and ignorant companion. When I had a companion we were both young and ignorant. I bit him all the time. He never bit back, which was annoying, though I now understand it as showing that he was more advanced in the Foundational Deliberation than I. The good die young. Perhaps to you, an advanced Practicant, biting is on the same low order as saying phhht? I hope not, as I still truly enjoy a good lightning bite every now and then. I was glad to find, however, while I was

carrying my mouse around, that my control was as good as ever; the mouse was entirely undamaged. And how did the humans receive this careful, thoughtful presentation, when it got up and ran off? With shrieks and lamentation! I shall never understand them.

May the food of Opal taste ever better to the Aunt of Opal.

And if, as I think may be, you are about to go into the House of Exile, may your time in the Horrible Carrier be brief, and may your mastery of all Five Deliberations make your time there pass like the dream of a winter's night.

Remotely,

Zorro

Dear Zorro,

There are things I do not understand.

My human is sitting (of which I approve). She has been sitting most of the day (better still). She is working with her tablet that vibrates and emits light and occasionally noises — I know you must know whereof I speak, these tablets seem to accompany most humans — and of course I help her. I keep her lap suitably warm, and when her tension level or my desire to snack rises beyond a certain level, I invoke Sameness, distract her and reestablish balance. I am used to her sometimes irritable responses to this and I do not mind them because they always eventually result in my getting what I want.

All of this is well known. The part I do not understand is her consistent failure to understand and appreciate my artistic applications of the Fourth Deliberation tail techniques. Over time I have practiced the artistic tail placements designed to enhance the beauty and useful-ness of any work surface, duly adapted to the tablet: Tip Rests on Delete Key; Delicately Brushing Trackpad; and so on.

Today, to honor her for spending such an unusually long time so nicely seated, I invoked the rare and exquisite Full Length Cross Keyboard Adornment. She was *utterly unappreciative*. Indeed I found myself summarily upon the floor, as if I were a mere kitten. I was quite offended ... I wondered whether you had had any similar rebuffs and how you dealt with them.

Fredi

P.S. Now, however, I am doing it again and she is letting me, by typing gently around and beneath my tail ... perhaps progress can be made after all. Persistence and steadfastness are key.

Zorro to Fredi

Dear Fredi,

Some time ago you wrote me a letter, which I apologise for not replying to sooner, concerning your human's odd behaviour in relation to your refined application of Fourth Deliberation Tail Technique.

I should shrug (if I had shoulders to shrug with) and dismiss this as typical human lack of appreciation of many applications of the Fourth Deliberation — such as their objection to one's gracefully sudden Placement between their face and a book or newspaper, their resistance to proper Bed Feng Shui arrangements, etc. — if it did not concern the tail.

I have a great interest in tail management. My tail is one of my best attributes. I carry it rather low, lion style. It is not full and fluffy, of course; I pride myself on my shorthair ancestry. It is very long, very black, very flexible, and I employ it with immense variety and eloquence.

My female has, I am happy to say, a quite admirable admiration of my tail, and distinctly appreciates its rhetorical and ornamental flourishes, as well as some of its subtler Placements, such as the slow draw across the cheek when napping, and the evanescent wrap about the leg when requesting treats.

Obviously, your tail, like mine, is faultless. Therefore I wonder if the problem is with the tablet, rather than with the tail?

The tablet is, I have come to believe, a very evil creature. It is not alive, but it definitely has powers — not crude ones, such as the horrible Vacuum Monster, which destroys one's self-possession by mere roaring and bellowing as it runs about — but subtle powers, to which the humans become deeply in thrall. It absorbs their energies in a strange way, leading them to ignore even Us.

I have found the wisest course to be total avoidance of the tablet. I do not set paw upon it even when it is shut up like a box. I do not attempt to sit upon the female when the tablet is casting its spell of vibrations, lights, and clicking noises on her. If I want something while she is under the tablet spell, I walk around and around her chair, using the delicate and charming evanescent tail wraps I mentioned above, leaning warmly against her legs, purring ostentatiously, looking up sweetly, etc.

If this does not work, and such is the malign power of the tablet, it often doesn't, then I unsheath. I begin to scratch alternately at her pants leg (very lightly) and on the wall next to her (rather loudly). I believe you use this latter technique on the headboard of her bed when she is violating Bed Feng Shui? It is quite effective, is it not? After a while she always hisses and gets up and goes downstairs to serve me my Soupy Supper so that I can ignore it for several hours before I eat it in the middle of the night.

You might try this form of Placement in order to obtain your wishes. But I am so sorry your female does not properly appreciate your tail. It is very sad.

Remotely Yours,

Zorro

Zorro to Opal

Dear Young Opal,

I don't know why it is, but you bring out something feral in me and so I have been wanting to ask you if you get violent impulses that overwhelm you so that you just go and do them?

The female human was petting my wonderfully thick, dense, silky, warm fur and I was purring away in full observation of the Third and Fifth Deliberations, when like lightning the desire to bite came upon me, and like lightning I bit.

I have only two fangs ever since the table attacked me, but they are extremely effective fangs. It was a forearm slash. She hissed furiously and swatted my elegant, slender backside quite hard. It was almost a cat reflex — but she can't unsheath, so it did no harm. I hissed back at her, leapt off the bed, and departed with dignity, while she was still hissing and bleeding. I felt good about the whole thing. Do you ever do anything like this?

I scarcely want to ask Fredi. I am sure she always observes the Deliberations, and I have a feeling that this behavior is, somehow, not quite in accord with any of them.

Blackly, Your
Uncle Zorro

A surviving version of a sign that
hung outside the Le Guins's
front door for decades.

PLEASE
DON'T LET THE
CAT
OUT!!

POEMS

NINE LINES, AUGUST 9

The gold of evening is closing,
drawing in, tightening.
The light is losing. It is
a little frightening
how fast August goes.
Others have noticed this.
The cat on his concealed switchblade toes
comes by, and what he says
is silent, but enlightening.

MAY 22

I will spend four days
writing love songs
in a house that's near
but doesn't look at
the sea.
   The first
is to the cat Archibald,
the demure, ceremonious,
innocent, elegant archer
of back, bestower
of affection from aloofness,
too young in wisdom
of death and people:
Mischief, Slantways,
devoutly greedy, gaze of amber,
erratic and indolent silk sherpa
to holy wholly mysterious everests,
I make a lovesong to him,
a gift, a dreamfeather.

I THINK OF THEM

all, their beautiful eyes,
gold and green-gold and beryl,
soft paces, silent presences,
the tail drawn across the wrist,
caress and blessing, the resolute
pursuit of comfort. All the floor
invisibly innumerably patterned
with four-petaled flowers. Laurel
crouched in the dignity of his agony
purring when I petted him.
Young Lorenzo poised cocky on a perilous
branch. A carton boiling over
with kittens, forty years ago. All the air
alive with ghostly leaps. We share the bed
with still, companionable warmths
through nights of how many winters
gone, dark now, and yet to darken.

GRACE

The kitten no bigger than a teacup growls
true threat at interference with his food,
will bite the hand that feeds him, and draw blood.
They are entire tiger in their souls.
They shame the monkeyness in us, that howls
and grins and chatters and knowing bad from good
claims to be other than the animals
and nearer than the tiger to the grace of God.

RAKSHA

I think I could turn and live with animals, they are so
placid and self-contain'd . . .
Not one is respectable or unhappy over the whole earth . . .
                    —Walt Whitman, "Song of Myself"

It's raining pretty hard in San Jose
and it has been raining
and will rain till late April, early May.
It isn't cold here. Only wet.
Rain pelting on the roofless porch.
Under the bushes by the porch is mud,
the parking lot is pools on asphalt,
the lawn is grassroots in water.
She can't get underneath the porch
so she gets underneath the chair.
An old green-plastic-covered armchair
too wide for the front door
sits mildewing inwardly
in the porch corner,
and the cat hides under it
from the rain. From loud noises.
From people in the parking lot.
From dogs and cars and me.

She lived in this apartment before I did.
When her people left,
the woman upstairs says,
they couldn't find her so they left her.
She's a left cat. Sinister.

Piercing eyes. Demonic. Scruffy, longhaired,
black. All black. Hisses, spits, and runs away.
Bites, they tell me. Hasn't bitten me,
I don't wait to get bitten. But she flinches,
flattens, if I touch her fur
however lightly, furtively,
a foolish bid for bonding,
when I put down the bowl she runs to
fearful, distrustful, but hungry, hungry.
Wet, cold, alone, and hungry.
That's a cat's life, Walt.

I guess she chose to stay here.
Hid from her people. *Kitty-kitty-kitty,*
the car all packed — *Come on kitty,*
swing from the branches with us happy simians!
No, the cat said. No.
I know my place.

I call her Raksha, demon,
but she has no name.

I leave the door wide.
She does not come in.
Self-contained, but never placid,
she crouches near her refuge chair,
even in her sleep alert, aware.
I can't judge if she is or is not unhappy.
She's certainly unlucky,
less so than many cats.
She accepts, she does not beg.
She is wholly respectable.

While I'm here to feed her twice a day
she has some ease. When I'm gone,
if the next tenant doesn't,
well, she'll get bone-thin again,
get lame again, get sick and hide and die.
Or a car or a dog will kill her.

Turn as we may in our wonderful ease-making words,
we cannot co-opt her freedom.
We can live with her
only on her hard terms.

MORNING IN JOSEPH, OREGON

Its shadow briefly tracks a starling's flight
across the dotted line that shows the way
a cat went straight across the snowy lawn
last night when just past full the sinking moon
cast shadows eastward in the silent town
and turned the snow peaks ashen grey.

Sun shines, bird flies, snow melts, the cat is gone.

DOGGEREL FOR MY CAT

His paws are white, his ears are black.
When he isn't around I feel the lack.
His purr is loud, his fur is soft.
He always carries his tail aloft.
His gait is easy, his gaze intense.
He wears a tuxedo to all events.
His toes are prickly, his nose is pink.
I like to watch him sit and think.
His breed is Alley, his name is Pard.
Life without him would be hard.

WRITTEN IN THE DARK

The lionesses of the mind are dangerous.
Big sinuous dun bodies range
the plains of sleep. The fangs are sharp.
The fire-yellow eyes fix on my heart.

PARD'S APPAREL

He wears a striking suit of black:
Long sleeves in front — short pants in back.
White is his tie, and white his shirt,
Immaculate of stain or dirt.
On his white stockings, from the rear,
Two ornamental spots appear,
Serving to lessen the albedo
Of his unusual tuxedo.

Lorenzo on my lap
11 XI 86

THE CAT

He walks upon his paws
To the places that he goes,
Followed by his tail
And preceded by his nose.

He knows what he is doing.
He goes about his business.
He need not explain it.
He is being his isness.

LULLABY

where's my little fleeting cat
a year a year an hour a day
where's my little girl at
fleeting away sleeping away
found the way clear away
nowhere far nowhere near
a day a day an hour a year

COMPANY

A paw, a questing nose half waken me,
and I let him get under the covers.
He curls up and purrs himself asleep.
Cats are less troublesome than lovers.

THE LIVES OF URSULA'S CATS

ANON, TICKIE, NERO, AND FIGARO (c. 1930–1940)
Photos from Ursula's first decade suggest that cats were part of her life from the time she could walk. It seems they may have been residents of Kishamish, the farmhouse where the Kroeber family spent each summer from 1930 onward; old albums show Ursula from about age 2 to 9 petting and holding different kittens and cats there, some of whose names are labeled and all of whom look possibly related, since they are all either black or black-and-white shorthairs—perhaps establishing the roots of her partiality for tuxedos.

PIFFLE (c. 1940–1947)
Sharp ears, short legs, as big, strong and grey as a battleship. He was dignified, but lived most of his life in the kitchen and ate as much food as you would give him, provided that he liked it. Carried on his duels of honor on the back lawn; he made love, however, for blocks around. He had no sense of humor, but he was a gentleman.

GASPAR (1952–c. 1954)
A playful and insouciant longhair gray tabby, Gaspar seems to have been the cat Ursula reluctantly left behind in Berkeley with her parents when she headed to France, where she would soon meet Charles and begin a new life, with (soon) new cats.

ANONYMOUS ILL-FATED KITTEN, AKA "CATFOOD" (c. 1959, LESS THAN A YEAR)

Tabby kitten, of uncertain origins, infested with fleas. (First Portland household cat! Tremendous excitement!) Elisabeth, age two, dissuaded from giving it the sublime name of Catfood, surely not for esthetic reasons but because there was some doubt as to whether it would live. Indeed it didn't for very long. (A flying-kitten experiment, undertaken off the back verandah, probably did not help.)

TOM AND TABBY (EARLY TO MID-1960s)

The first generation of "Bates' Cats," named for family friends who raised large, dignified, long-haired orange cats. Tom was indeed a tomcat, prone to fighting and abscessed ears and spraying to mark his territory; Tabby was a momma cat. They lived largely outside, being put out at night and allowed back inside in the morning through a clattery cat door Charles cut into the back porch. Both retired to country life when the family was away from home for a year.

LAUREL (c. 1965–c. 1973)

A large long-haired marmalade gentleman; elegant, independent, and affectionate. Caroline wanted to name him Pinky, for his pink paw pads; this was vetoed by Ursula, who suggested the comic actor duo as namesakes for both Laurel and his brother Hardy, who was the darker orange and stockier of the two. Both were second-generation "Bates" cats and like their uncle Tom, they were prone to spraying, much to Charles's ire ("damn cats").

HARDY (c. 1965–1970)

Hardy was a fine specimen of ginger catness, robust, the swirls of his long tabby coat a vivid dark orange. He took his territorial duties seriously, often going out on patrol, and sometimes suffered injuries in the line of duty.

Neko

NEKO (c. 1970–c. 1988)

A muddled grey/orange tortoiseshell, Neko may have been the original ballooncat. She had a large round body, a small head, small feet, small tail, and a small squeaky meow. Ursula said of her that she lacked tact — she had a way of gracelessly and clumsily inserting herself onto laps, beds, and underfoot. The longest-lived of all the Le Guin cats and perhaps the least charismatic, outliving several stronger characters, until one day at eighteen she simply disappeared — returned to her people, it was said.

Leonard

LEONARD (1974–c. 1988)

A long-haired black-and white kitten, lost and bewildered in the hullabaloo of the Portland Rose Parade, rescued and named by Dorothy Hirsch, Elisabeth's best friend at school. Leonard moved into the Thurman Street house as to the manor born and enjoyed a long reign. When not occupied with the many pressing concerns of the nobility, he made contributions to science, notably inspiring Ursula's Theory of Feline Gravitational Conservation: the mass conserved by an ascending feline (viz., feather-light arrival of fourteen-pound animal on kitchen counter) is doubled upon its descent (viz., leaden thump, as of twenty-eight-pound sandbag, when obliged by cook to jump off said counter).

MISS MOPPET (1978–1979)
Tiny, beautiful, and doomed, Miss Moppet immigrated from Napa Valley to Portland and lived scarcely a year, breaking the hearts of all.

Philip

PHILIP (1979–c. 1993)
Handsome, kind, heroic in profile, but a bit of a dim bulb compared to his smaller brother Lorenzo. Many royal families have this fraternal juxtaposition — the noble and dignified elder, destined to rule or die young, and the scamp who manages to steal the limelight and avoid duty.

Bonzo

LORENZO, AKA BONZO (1979–c. 1996)

A small neat classic tabby, with small white paws and a
white nose, littermate of Philip, and generational relation
to Miss Moppet — all three the kittens of Mother
Courage, the partly tame momma cat who raised her litters
under the house at Kishamish in Napa Valley for several
summers. Lorenzo was almost not adopted (Philip had
already been selected), but Caroline insisted with tears
he too must join the family, leading to the era of a four-cat
house. Lorenzo's intelligence, wit, and self-possession
soon charmed and mastered all inhabitants of the house,
Charles included.

ARCHIE AND WILLIE (c. 1997–1998)

After the end of the four-cat era, two pale-orange and
white little brothers came into the household as sickly
kittens already infected with feline leukemia. For their
too-short lives they were loved and nursed and worried
over by Ursula and by Charles, who was continuing his
journey to becoming a cat person.

ZORRO (LATE 1998–2011)

After Willie died, Ursula asked her vet to let her know
if anybody left a kitten at the veterinary door. The next
morning the vet called: Zorro had been left on her
doorstep. Zorro always wore a tuxedo. He was a great
mouser, but more detective than killer; most of the mice
were left, if not entirely intact, at least alive. His tail was

a great asset to interspecies communication. Long for his size, with it he expressed emotions, dissatisfactions, and needs quite eloquently without resorting to vocalization.

PARDO, AKA PARD (2011–PRESENT)

At the Humane Society, Pard chose Ursula. Another tuxedo wearer, pretty according to Ursula, with eyes of alexandrite, changing color according to the angle of the light. As his arrival coincided with the early days of Ursula's blog, much ink was spilled in chronicling his early life. Persistent, curious, and buoyant, Pard is adept in door-opening, vase-overturning, and improbably high-surface visitation. He was always most comfortable with Ursula but has proven himself adaptable in upper-middle age. Though skittish of most people and especially men early on, he spent a good part of his middle age on the lap of Charles (completing Charles's journey to becoming a cat person). Like Zorro, a Great Hunter but unable to make the kill. As Ursula wrote, "his instincts and skills are impeccably feline, but his education was incomplete.

SOURCES & ACKNOWLEDGMENTS

The poems and other material comprising this volume are reprinted from the following sources. All drawings by Ursula K. Le Guin courtesy of The Ursula K. Le Guin Literary Trust.

Epigraph on page 2. "Cheek by Jowl: Animals in Children's Literature," *Cheek by Jowl* (Seattle: Aqueduct Press, 2009): 105.

The Art of Bunditsu (Seattle, WA: Ygor & Buntho Make Books Press, 1982).

"Black Leonard in Negative Space." *Buffalo Gals: And Other Animal Presences* (Santa Barbara: Capra Press, 1987): 152.

"For Leonard, Darko, and Burton Watson." *Buffalo Gals: And Other Animal Presences* (Santa Barbara: Capra Press, 1987): 154.

"Tabby Lorenzo." *Buffalo Gals: And Other Animal Presences* (Santa Barbara: Capra Press, 1987): 152.

"A Conversation with a Silence." *Buffalo Gals: And Other Animal Presences* (Santa Barbara: Capra Press, 1987): 153.

"Don Diego." Copyright © 2025 by The Ursula K. Le Guin Literary Trust.

"A Little Death." Copyright © 2025 by The Ursula K. Le Guin Literary Trust.

"I Think of Them." *Finding My Elegy: New and Selected Poems* (Boston: Houghton Mifflin Harcourt, 2012): 128.

"Grace." *Finding My Elegy: New and Selected Poems* (Boston: Houghton Mifflin Harcourt, 2012): 129.

"Raksha." *Finding My Elegy: New and Selected Poems* (Boston: Houghton Mifflin Harcourt, 2012): 130–32.

"Morning in Joseph, Oregon." *Finding My Elegy: New and Selected Poems* (Boston: Houghton Mifflin Harcourt, 2012): 140.

"Doggerel for My Cat." *No Time To Spare: Thinking About What Matters* (New York: Houghton Mifflin Harcourt, 2017): 154. Copyright © 2017 by Ursula K. Le Guin. Reprinted by permission of HarperCollins LLC.

"Written in the Dark." *Late in the Day: Poems 2010–2014* (Oakland, CA: PM Press, 2016): 37. Reprinted by permission of PM Press.

"Pard's Apparel." https://www.ursulakleguin.com/blog/117-health-update [accessed September 12, 2024].

"The Cat." *Love Can Be: A Literary Collection About Our Animals, ed. Louisa McCune and Teresa Miller* (Oklahoma City: Kirkpatrick Foundation, 2018): 7. Reprinted by permission of Kirkpatrick Foundation.

"Lullaby." *So Far So Good: Final Poems 2014–2018* (Port Townsend, WA: Copper Canyon, 2018): 17.

"Falling: Company." *So Far So Good: Final Poems 2014–2018* (Port Townsend, WA: Copper Canyon, 2018): 48.

Quotation on page 98. Postcard to Martha West [undated].

The *Catless* manuscript is *not* worth writing.

The text for *Ursula K. Le Guin's Book of Cats* is set in Louize, which French type designer Matthieu Cortat issued in 2013 as a contemporary reinterpretation of Augustaux, a nineteenth-century typeface issued under the guidance of Lyonnaisse printer Louis Perrin. The titles and running heads have been set in Diatype, a sans serif typeface released by Berlin-based type studio ABC Dinamo in 2020.

Text design and composition by Isabel Urbina Peña. Printing and binding by Sheridan in Brainerd, MN. The jacket was printed by Phoenix Color, a division of Lakeside Book Company. The books are bound in Allure, a polycotton blended cloth with an aqueous acrylic coating. The paper is acid-free and exceeds the requirements for permanence established by the American National Standards Institute.

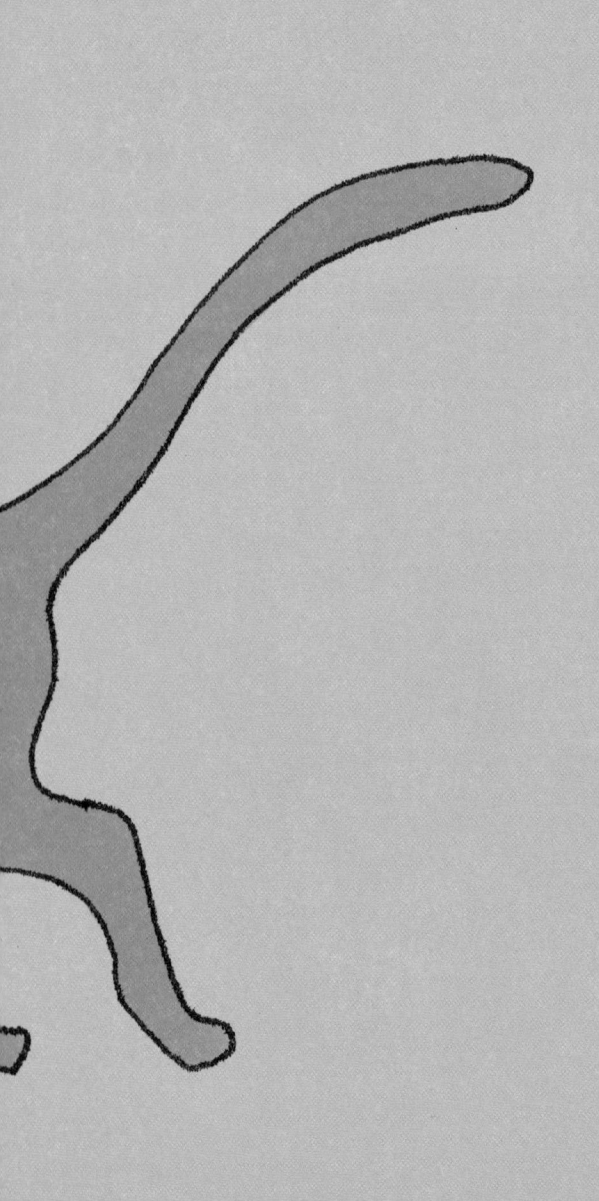